CELEBRATING HOLIDAYS

Martin Luther King, Jr. Day

by Rachel Grack

BLASTOFF! READERS
2

BELLWETHER MEDIA • MINNEAPOLIS, MN

Note to Librarians, Teachers, and Parents:

Blastoff! Readers are carefully developed by literacy experts and combine standards-based content with developmentally appropriate text.

Level 1 provides the most support through repetition of high-frequency words, light text, predictable sentence patterns, and strong visual support.

Level 2 offers early readers a bit more challenge through varied simple sentences, increased text load, and less repetition of high-frequency words.

Level 3 advances early-fluent readers toward fluency through increased text and concept load, less reliance on visuals, longer sentences, and more literary language.

Level 4 builds reading stamina by providing more text per page, increased use of punctuation, greater variation in sentence patterns, and increasingly challenging vocabulary.

Level 5 encourages children to move from "learning to read" to "reading to learn" by providing even more text, varied writing styles, and less familiar topics.

Whichever book is right for your reader, Blastoff! Readers are the perfect books to build confidence and encourage a love of reading that will last a lifetime!

This edition first published in 2018 by Bellwether Media, Inc.

No part of this publication may be reproduced in whole or in part without written permission of the publisher. For information regarding permission, write to Bellwether Media, Inc., Attention: Permissions Department, 5357 Penn Avenue South, Minneapolis, MN 55419.

Library of Congress Cataloging-in-Publication Data

Names: Koestler-Grack, Rachel A., 1973- author.
Title: Martin Luther King, Jr. Day / by Rachel Grack.
Description: Minneapolis, MN : Bellwether Media, Inc., [2018] | Series:
   Blastoff! Readers: Celebrating Holidays | Includes bibliographical
   references and index. | Audience: Grades K-3. | Audience: Ages 5-8.
Identifiers: LCCN 2017029516 | ISBN 9781626177529 (hardcover : alk. paper) | ISBN 9781681034577 (ebook)
Subjects: LCSH: Martin Luther King, Jr.–Day–Juvenile literature. | King, Martin Luther, Jr., 1929-1968–Juvenile literature. |
   African Americans–Civil rights–History–20th century–Juvenile literature. | African American civil rights workers–
   Biography–Juvenile literature. | Civil rights workers–United States–Biography–Juvenile literature.
Classification: LCC E185.97.K5 K58 2018 | DDC 394.261–dc23
LC record available at https://lccn.loc.gov/2017029516

Editor: Paige V. Polinsky   Designer: Lois Stanfield

Printed in the United States of America, North Mankato, MN.

Table of Contents

Martin Luther King, Jr. Day Is Here!

Children and parents
feed the hungry.

Martin Luther King, Jr.
Memorial in
Washington, D.C.

They honor one brave man who
risked his life to help others. It is
Martin Luther King, Jr. Day!

What Is Martin Luther King, Jr. Day?

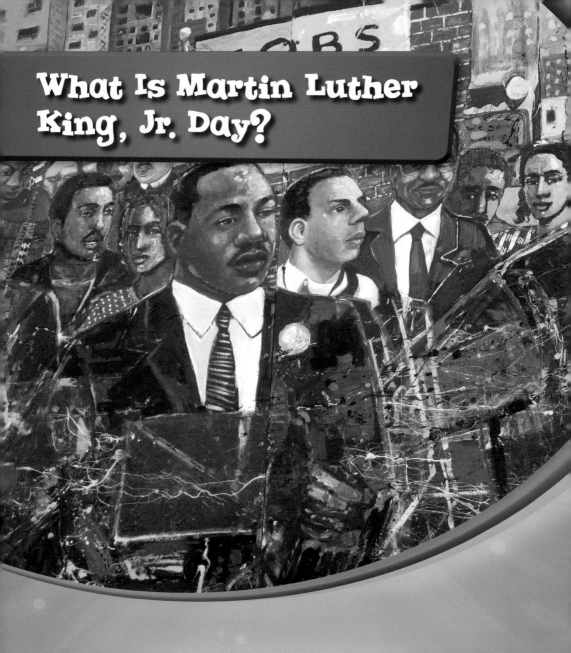

This holiday celebrates the **civil rights** leader Martin Luther King, Jr.

He used peaceful **protests** to end **discrimination**. His work changed the world!

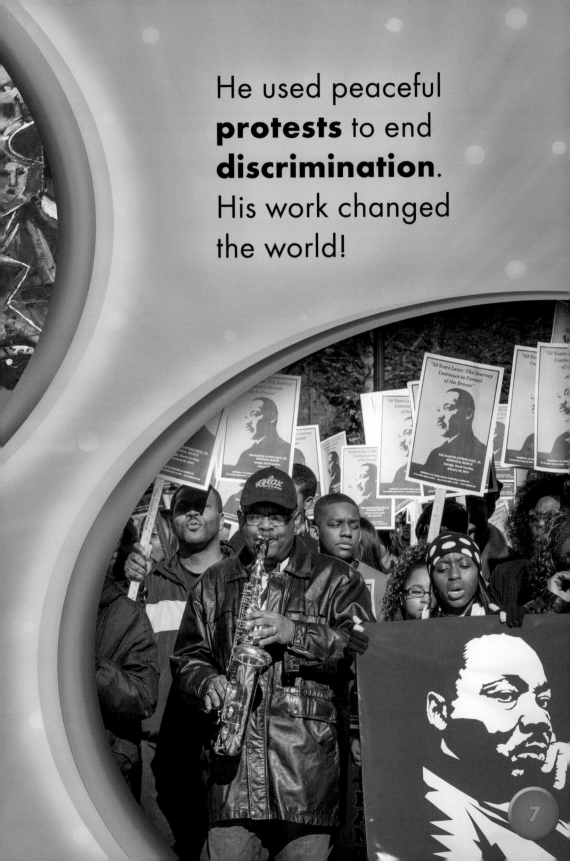

Who Celebrates Martin Luther King, Jr. Day?

The United States celebrates **equality** for all people on this holiday.

Some states call it Civil Rights Day or Equality Day.

segregation

Americans have struggled to treat each other equally. Different **races** were even **segregated** on buses.

Starting in 1955, King led a bus **boycott** in Montgomery, Alabama. This helped end segregation.

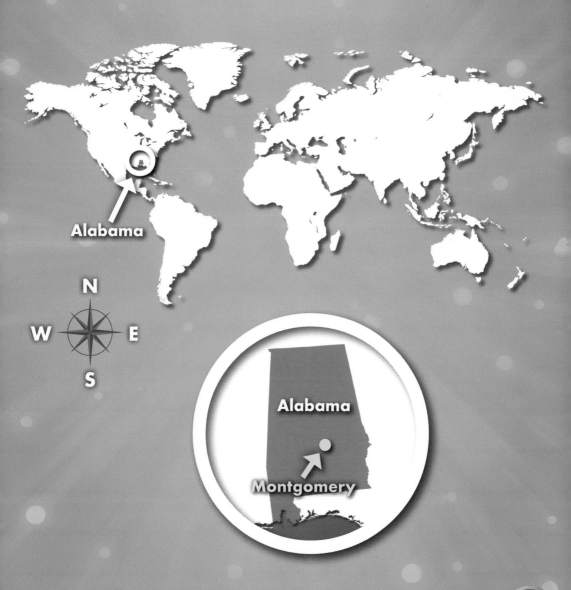

Alabama

N
W E
S

Alabama

Montgomery

Martin Luther King, Jr.

King led the March on Washington in 1963. More than 200,000 people gathered to hear his **speech**, "I Have a Dream." His protests brought new laws. These laws supported civil rights.

Make a Handprint Wreath

This wreath shows how all hands can work together for equality!

What You Need:

- paper plate
- scissors
- colored construction paper
- pencil
- glue stick
- hole punch
- ribbon, 24 inches long

What You Do:

1. Cut out the center of the plate, leaving a 2-inch ring.
2. Trace about 20 handprints on paper.
3. Cut out each handprint.
4. Glue handprints to the ring with fingers pointing outward.
5. Punch a hole in the ring.
6. Fold the ribbon in half. Pull the folded end halfway through the hole on the ring's front side. Tie the ends in a bow on the back side of the wreath.
7. Use the ribbon loop to hang your wreath!

1

4

3

6

**President
Ronald Reagan**

In 1968, King was shot and killed. Many people wanted a holiday to honor his life.

President Ronald Reagan created a **national** holiday in 1983.

Martin Luther King, Jr. and Civil Rights

1955	Montgomery Bus Boycott begins
1963	King leads the March on Washington
1964	Civil Rights Act passes; King wins the Nobel Peace Prize.
1965	Voting Rights Act passes

A Day to Honor

Martin Luther King, Jr. Day takes place on the third Monday in January.

REV. MARTIN LUTHER KING. JR.
1929 — 1968

"Free at last. Free at last.
Thank God Almighty
I'm Free at last."

It falls on or near King's birthday, January 15.

Martin Luther King, Jr. Day Traditions!

People **volunteer** in their **communities** on this day. They help the homeless and care for others in need.

Some cities hold parades.

It is a day to honor equality.

A DAY ON...NOT A DAY OFF
REMEMBER! CELEBRATE! ACT!
JANUARY 15, 2001
MARTIN LUTHER
KING JR.

People remember Martin Luther King, Jr.'s work for civil rights. They celebrate his life!

Glossary

boycott—an event in which people refuse to buy or do something

civil rights—the rights all people have to freedom and equal treatment under the law

communities—places where people live together

discrimination—the act of treating someone unfairly because of race, gender, age, or other differences

equality—the same rights for everyone

national—related to the entire country

protests—events held to show people are against something

races—groups of humans that share common backgrounds

segregated—kept apart based on race; segregation was common in the United States until the 1960s.

speech—a talk given to a group of people

volunteer—to offer to do a job without pay

To Learn More

AT THE LIBRARY

Herrington, Lisa M. *Martin Luther King Jr. Day.* New York, N.Y.: Children's Press, 2013.

Jazynka, Kitson. *Martin Luther King, Jr.* Washington, D.C.: National Geographic, 2012.

Rappaport, Doreen. *Martin's Big Words: The Life of Dr. Martin Luther King, Jr.* New York, N.Y.: Hyperion, 2007.

ON THE WEB

Learning more about Martin Luther King, Jr. Day is as easy as 1, 2, 3.

1. Go to www.factsurfer.com.

2. Enter "Martin Luther King, Jr. Day" into the search box.

3. Click the "Surf" button and you will see a list of related web sites.

With factsurfer.com, finding more information is just a click away.

Index

The images in this book are reproduced through the courtesy of: kropic1, front cover; Steve Debenport, p. 4; stock_photo_world, p. 5; By Forty3Zero, p. 6; EPG_EuroPhotoGraphics, pp. 7, 8, 19; Frances Roberts/ Alamy, pp. 9, 20; Horace Cort/ AP Images p. 10; Francis Miller/ Getty Images, p. 12; Tamara JM Peterson/ Bellwether Media, p. 13 (all); White House Photo/ Alamy, p. 14; sun7, pp. 15, 22; Joseph Becker, p. 16; David Grossman/ Alamy, p. 17; RosaIreneBetancourt 7/ Alamy, p. 18; Xinhua/ Alamy, p. 21.